Poets From London
Edited By Sarah Olivo

First published in Great Britain in 2019 by:

Young Writers
Remus House
Coltsfoot Drive
Peterborough
PE2 9BF
Telephone: 01733 890066
Website: www.youngwriters.co.uk

All Rights Reserved
Book Design by Spencer Hart
© Copyright Contributors 2019
Softback ISBN 978-1-78988-899-7
Hardback ISBN 978-1-83928-547-9
Printed and bound in the UK by BookPrintingUK
Website: www.bookprintinguk.com
YB0419J

Foreword

Dear Reader,

Are you ready to explore the wonderful delights of poetry?

Young Writers' *Poetry Patrol* gang set out to encourage and ignite the imaginations of 5-7 year-olds as they took their first steps into the magical world of poetry. With **Riddling Rabbit**, **Acrostic Croc** and **Sensory Skunk** on hand to help, children were invited to write an acrostic, sense poem or riddle on any theme, from people to places, animals to objects, food to seasons. *Poetry Patrol* is also a great way to introduce children to the use of poetic expression, including onomatopoeia and similes, repetition and metaphors, acting as stepping stones for their future poetic journey.

All of us here at Young Writers believe in the importance of inspiring young children to produce creative writing, including poetry, and we feel that seeing their own poem in print will keep that creative spirit burning brightly and proudly.

We hope you enjoy reading this wonderful collection as much as we enjoyed reading all the entries.

Contents

Argyle Primary School, Camden

Maddalena Opocher (6)	1
Sabrina Yasmin (6)	2
Akirah Gray (6)	3

Ark Byron Primary Academy, Acton

Jemma Hall (6)	4
Mateo Webb (6)	5
Alyssa Sagoo (6)	6
Rita Durie (5)	7
Connor Cowland (5)	8

Azhar Academy, Leytonstone

Zeynep Gencer (5)	9
Abdullah R (6)	10
Aisha Samater (6)	11
Aisha Hajee (5)	12
Hafsah Tailor (6)	13
Ayoub Azzouz (6)	14
Maryam Imran Patel (6)	15
Aisha Hussain (6)	16
Musa Ahmed (6)	17
Aadam Ubayd Hasnat (6)	18
Abdullah Muhammad Azeem (5)	19
Aaminah Hajee (6)	20
Juwairiah Rahman (6)	21

Buttercup Primary School, Whitechapel

Simrah Yasmin Faruque (6)	22
Musa Manik (8)	23
Mariam Liloul (7)	24
Zahra Malaika Emran (7)	25
Muhammed Yunus (7)	26
Humaira Kona (6)	27
Amirah Ahmed (7)	28
Nishatjahan Mahmud (6)	29
Talhah Allen (8)	30

Gainsborough Primary School, London

Emile Talavichute (6)	31
Xarissa Dopwell (5)	32
Sudais Mohammed (6)	33
Zaynab Mohamed (6)	34
Elizabeth Tothill (6)	35
Patricia Esohe Irabor (6)	36
Emmanuel Ntiamoah (6)	37
Abdul Zahir (6)	38
Sarah St Ange (6)	39

Holmleigh Primary School, Hackney

Mia Chia-White (6)	40
Nathen Yeboah (6)	41
Sophia Abels Martí (6)	42
Daniel Ogu (5)	43
Muhammad-Suhayb Ibn Ahmed Muhammad (6)	44

Lalibela-Rose Monica Jones-Thomas (5)	45
Lukas Kollewe-Robinson (6)	46
Rasharn Smith (6)	47
Zion-Leigh Jonah Wallace (6)	48
Raphael Opoku (6)	49
Ziyad Rawat (5)	50
Haseeb Siddique (6)	51
Essa Muruts (5)	52
Izan Fitzpatrick Salazar (5)	53
Nathan Okulo Nugent (6)	54

Mayville Primary School, Leytonstone

Michelle Oke (6)	55
Carolina Valentina Pacheco Rich (7)	56
Amelia Niemira (7)	58
Yousuf Muhammad (7)	59

Noel Park Primary School, Wood Green

Kimperly Boulou (7)	60
Emilia Kasiak (7)	61
Larisa Diana Dorcu (6)	62
Jennica Sustines (7)	63
Elisaveta Ilieva (7)	64
Liliana Ryzner (7)	65
Alex Harding (6)	66
Imani Ahmed (6)	67

Our Lady Of Lourdes Catholic Primary School, Finchley

Michele Zeolla (6)	68
Adela Mladenova (6)	69
Liana Dzadonova-Soskova (6)	70

Randal Cremer Primary School, Hackney

Houh Keskinbicak (7)	72
Finlay Dudek-Mahon (6)	74
Mani George Lister (6)	75
Kayden Tayvon Davis (6)	76
Yusuf Ahmed	77
Harry Paul Johns (5)	78
Mustafa Mohamed (6)	79
Rafael Silva Amorim (6)	80
Olusegun Isaiah Olaifa (7)	81
Mariyah Rahman (6)	82

Seven Sisters Primary School, Tottenham

Khalid Ainab (6)	83
Kerenza-Gabbie Alexiah Guei Nguiladjoe (6)	84
Ayaan Abdul (6)	85
Elalavin Toraman (6)	86
Emma Emmanuel (6)	87

St Joseph's RC Primary School, Willesden

Miguel Dalfior-Milanese (6)	88
Elijah Monu (5)	89
Leandra Aragao (6)	90
Joseph O'Connor-Macklen (6)	91
Lexi Carrido (5)	92
Adam Stachowicz (6)	93
Mila Ndidi Aurora Johnson (6)	94
Cristian Alcantara (6)	95
Yafet Michael (6)	96
Zenaye Richards (6)	97
Kojo Agbugba (6)	98
Angel Mabag (6)	99
Diane Omas (6)	100
Zackary Resurreccion Geluz Silva (6)	101
Nicole Ferreira (6)	102
Remy Kyerematen (6)	103
Zuzanna Baran (6)	104

Sara Bereket (6)	105
Molly Noonan-Conneely (6)	106
Jean Alexander Calva Angeles (6)	107
Sarah Lukowska (6)	108
Liliana Czapska (6)	109
Chanelle Cadigal Bernardo (6)	110
Tristan Mingo Corpuz (6)	111
Bethany Elfy (6)	112
Taira Miankanina (6)	113
Julio Peixoto Jr (6)	114
Bezawit-Elen Berhane (6)	115
Roxy Ayisi (5)	116
Althea Megan Matysik (5)	117
Lily-Sue O'Dea Nolan (6)	118
Chloe Pereira de Jesus (6)	119
Marcel Oliwkiewicz (6)	120
Mia-Rose Berry (5)	121
Ionna Braganca (6)	122
Anaise Toyin Amiyah Allen (6)	123
Oliwer Kwasniak (6)	124
Thiery Daisy (6)	125
Bleu-Taneil Henry-Skye (6)	126
Amelia-Mae Norwood (6)	127
Renee Labiran (6)	128
Isabella Lynn-Lee-Henningham (6)	129
Amelia Grace Myers (6)	130
Maxymilian Olczyk-Pinto (6)	131
Antoni Sagalski (6)	132
Da'Shaun Brown (5)	133
Urte Raubaite (5)	134
Sergio Santos Filho (5)	135
Marie Gilera (6)	136
Roukai Edwards (6)	137
Karina Firlej (6)	138
Janiah Hall (5)	139
James Koroma (6)	140
Colm O'Brien (6)	141

St Jude & St Paul's CE Primary School, London

Daniel Lahuk (7)	142
Teniola Aluko (7)	143
Kaylie Evans (7)	144

St Mary's CE Primary School, Stoke Newington

Tina David (7)	145

The Holmewood School, Barnet

Tomisin Okotore (10)	146

Upton Meadows Primary School, Upton

Raafay Yusuf (7)	147
Nehal Ba Omar (7)	148

Vita Et Pax School, Southgate

Megan Wilson (6)	149

Wimbledon Common Preparatory School, Wimbledon

Kiaan Mukherjee (6)	150
Atharva Sharma (6)	151
Isaiah van der Meer (7)	152
Kevin Ruo (7)	153

The Poems

Raindrops

Once there were two raindrops
She was called Shine
And he was called Dark
She was shiny blue and he was dark purple

She went up, he went down
How different they are!
In summer, she went down
In winter, he went down

She was happy, but he was sad
I can't meet the boy
But I can meet the girl
Who can you meet?

Maddalena Opocher (6)
Argyle Primary School, Camden

Little Bird

Birds soar in my garden
With animals like other birds
However, my neighbours don't like birds
at all!
They fuss about everything, even if there is
no reason
But now they have calmed down.

Sabrina Yasmin (6)
Argyle Primary School, Camden

Whose Sleigh?

I have a reindeer
It is brown
I have a white and red coat
I have a beard
It is white
I deliver toys and the reindeer flies.
Who am I?

Answer: I am Santa!

Akirah Gray (6)
Argyle Primary School, Camden

At The Beach

When I am at the beach, I feel...
Soft sand tickling my feet
Cool breeze on my face
Warm sand on my back
The sound of the waves
And the clicking and clacking of the shells swept up by the waves.

Jemma Hall (6)
Ark Byron Primary Academy, Acton

King Cobra!

K ing Cobra is very scary
I reland is King Cobra's favourite place
N ew Zealand is where King Cobra was born
G iraffes are King Cobra's favourite things to eat.

Mateo Webb (6)
Ark Byron Primary Academy, Acton

Tomorrow

Tomorrow, I'm going to bake a biscuit
Make up a magic trick
Kick a kangaroo
Ride on a rhino
Jump on a giraffe
I'm going to be so busy, I'll need a nap!
But when?

Alyssa Sagoo (6)
Ark Byron Primary Academy, Acton

Flowers Bloom

Flowers bloom all the time,
When you see a flower, don't pick it up,
It is there to see,
I love flowers, flowers are beautiful,
Flowers, flowers, flowers!

Rita Durie (5)
Ark Byron Primary Academy, Acton

I Am Smart

I am smart
And I drive a cart
My name is Mart
In fact, I am very smart
I built my cart
That's why I'm smart.

Connor Cowland (5)
Ark Byron Primary Academy, Acton

Roses
Haiku poetry

Roses are pretty.
Roses come out in summer.
Roses like sunlight.

Roses are silk-soft.
Roses are like fluffy clouds.
Roses are lovely.

Zeynep Gencer (5)
Azhar Academy, Leytonstone

Frogs
A haiku

Frogs have spotty legs.
Frogs have very smooth bodies.
Frogs have long red tongues.

Abdullah R (6)
Azhar Academy, Leytonstone

Bubble
A haiku

I love finding fish
I love the way they bubble
Bubble, bubble, pop!

Aisha Samater (6)
Azhar Academy, Leytonstone

Trees
A haiku

Trees are brown and green.
I see trees in the forest.
There are spiky trees.

Aisha Hajee (5)
Azhar Academy, Leytonstone

Rabbits
A haiku

Rabbits are cuddly
They have really fluffy fur
They have cute, small ears.

Hafsah Tailor (6)
Azhar Academy, Leytonstone

The Star
A haiku

The star is so soft.
The star is red and so bright.
The star is shining.

Ayoub Azzouz (6)
Azhar Academy, Leytonstone

Roses
A haiku

Roses make me calm.
There are many different kinds.
They are beautiful.

Maryam Imran Patel (6)
Azhar Academy, Leytonstone

The Roses
A haiku

The roses are soft.
They are beautiful and smooth.
They are so prickly.

Aisha Hussain (6)
Azhar Academy, Leytonstone

Flowers
A haiku

Flowers are so smooth.
They are very soft and sharp.
It is very light.

Musa Ahmed (6)
Azhar Academy, Leytonstone

Rainbow
A haiku

Colours are the best.
They always have lovely rays.
It is colourful.

Aadam Ubayd Hasnat (6)
Azhar Academy, Leytonstone

The Moon
A haiku

The moon is shining.
The moon has some sparkliness.
It is beautiful.

Abdullah Muhammad Azeem (5)
Azhar Academy, Leytonstone

Roses
A haiku

Roses have a stem.
Roses come out in summer.
Roses are spiky.

Aaminah Hajee (6)
Azhar Academy, Leytonstone

Roses
A haiku

Roses are yellow
Roses grow in the garden
They are beautiful.

Juwairiah Rahman (6)
Azhar Academy, Leytonstone

Princess

P rincesses are amazing, you know it
R emember Cinderella, whose gown doesn't fit?
I know all the Disney princesses
N ala and Pocahontas are princesses, did you know?
C inderella is as kind as a flower
E lsa is a frozen queen
S now White's lips are as red as a rose
S leeping Beauty is a total sleeper.

Simrah Yasmin Faruque (6)
Buttercup Primary School, Whitechapel

Kindness Is Love

K indness is truly love.
I like kindness and that's me.
N o one should be bullying.
D o not bully.
N o others are bullying so be kind.
E asy to be kind but hard to be bad.
S o be good and not bad.
S ave some time doing good stuff.

Musa Manik (8)
Buttercup Primary School, Whitechapel

Family Love

F un is when you spend time with your family
A dore is for loving each other
M atter, because they are important
I lluminate because they make me shine
L ove is because we learn to respect
Y ou because you love me no matter what.

Mariam Liloul (7)
Buttercup Primary School, Whitechapel

A Scary Visitor

I love stinky children
I do scary magic
I live in a scary, hairy cottage
I am a fairy who is scary
I eat stinky cherries
I wear wicked clothes
I eat wicked cheese
Who am I?

Answer: A wicked witch!

Zahra Malaika Emran (7)
Buttercup Primary School, Whitechapel

Sterling

Sterling, Sterling
Sterling on
When I play FIFA, Sterling is always on
Man City skills
Penalty shoot-out
Bang, bang! Perfect, perfect
I'm a fire-starter
I'm playing a season for no reason!

Muhammed Yunus (7)
Buttercup Primary School, Whitechapel

My Poem

I am a human
I love my family and friends and cousins
I read books
I wear clothes
I love to play
Do you love the world?
I love the world
Did you know that we have pipes
In our digestive system?

Humaira Kona (6)
Buttercup Primary School, Whitechapel

Summer

S unshine is so bright
U nder the burning heat
M any people are in many countries
M any times people are happy
E veryone loves the sun
R unning outside is good exercise.

Amirah Ahmed (7)
Buttercup Primary School, Whitechapel

Poem About My Family

F un activities with my family
A dventures we go on
M emorable moments we share
I nspired to be a good person
L ove, care and happiness
Y ay, I love my family!

Nishatjahan Mahmud (6)
Buttercup Primary School, Whitechapel

You

Y ou have power
O n the last day, you will get judged
U p in Heaven, you can do anything.

Talhah Allen (8)
Buttercup Primary School, Whitechapel

Seaside Summer

S unny, shiny waves
E veryone likes ice cream
A s you want ice cream, get it
S andcastles are fun
I ce cream is yellow and yummy
D elicious ice cream
E veryone likes super sandcastles.

Emile Talavichute (6)
Gainsborough Primary School, London

Seaside

S easide is fun, I like to make a castle.
E njoy the sea.
A pples are in my bag.
S alty sand.
I ce cream is at the seaside.
D ad is in the sea with me.
E njoy swimming.

Xarissa Dopwell (5)
Gainsborough Primary School, London

Seaside

S ea is wet.
E at an ice cream.
A dog is not allowed on the beach.
S ummer is hot.
I went into the water.
D oes the sea have water?
E at an apple at the beach.

Sudais Mohammed (6)
Gainsborough Primary School, London

The Seaside

S easide is fun
E xciting beach
A pples are supposed to be in your packed lunch
S ea is splashy
I ce cream is yummy
D irt in the sand
E njoy and have fun!

Zaynab Mohamed (6)
Gainsborough Primary School, London

Seaside

S easide is great!
E xciting things happen.
A n apple is in your hand.
S alty sea and sand.
I ce cream is nice.
D angerous sharks.
E njoy your day!

Elizabeth Tothill (6)
Gainsborough Primary School, London

Seaside Summer

S un cream.
E ating sticky sweets
A nd having perfect picnics.
S ummer is fun.
I ce cream is yummy.
D igging sandcastles.
E ating hot dogs.

Patricia Esohe Irabor (6)
Gainsborough Primary School, London

Seaside

S hiny sun
E ating hot dogs and sticky sweets
A good bouncing boat
S andcastles
I ce cream
D iving in the water
E ating ice cream.

Emmanuel Ntiamoah (6)
Gainsborough Primary School, London

Seaside

S ummer is fun.
E ggs are yummy.
A pples are yummy.
S ea is fun.
I ce cream is yummy.
D elivery pizza is yummy.
E njoy the view.

Abdul Zahir (6)
Gainsborough Primary School, London

Hot Sun

S un cream
E ating smooth sandwiches
A nd having burgers
S ummer is the best
I ce cream
D igging up soft sand
E at hot dogs.

Sarah St Ange (6)
Gainsborough Primary School, London

Family

My family looks like
Beautiful sunshine in the sky.
My family sounds like
A lily floating in the breeze.
My family tastes like
My home-made banana cake.
My family smells like candyfloss
And my grandmother's cuddles.

Mia Chia-White (6)
Holmleigh Primary School, Hackney

Lamborghini

My Lamborghini looks colourful.
My Lamborghini sounds like a rocket.
My Lamborghini tastes like a pear.
My Lamborghini smells like an engine.
My Lamborghini feels like a person
Giving me a hug.

Nathen Yeboah (6)
Holmleigh Primary School, Hackney

Climbing

Climbing looks very hard and dangerous.
Climbing sounds like beautiful fresh air.
Climbing tastes like wind and air.
Climbing smells sweaty and stinky.
Climbing feels like hard rocks.

Sophia Abels Martí (6)
Holmleigh Primary School, Hackney

Mummy

She looks like an angel.
She sounds like a beautiful song.
She tastes like cake.
She smells like a beautiful perfume.
She feels like soft and fluffy pillows.

Daniel Ogu (5)
Holmleigh Primary School, Hackney

Flowers

Flowers look like ladybirds
I hear flowers laughing
Flowers taste like blueberries
Flowers smell like watermelons
Flowers feel like fluffy cats.

Muhammad-Suhayb Ibn Ahmed Muhammad (6)
Holmleigh Primary School, Hackney

Summer

It looks like the beautiful sun
It sounds like the waves
It tastes like ice cream
It smells like fresh grass
It feels soft like a teddy.

Lalibela-Rose Monica Jones-Thomas (5)
Holmleigh Primary School, Hackney

My Birthday

It looks like flowers
It sounds like wrapping
It tastes like chocolate
It smells like apple juice
It feels like ripping open a present.

Lukas Kollewe-Robinson (6)
Holmleigh Primary School, Hackney

Football

It looks like my friends.
It sounds like lots of shouting.
It tastes like victory.
It smells like fresh green grass.
It feels rough.

Rasharn Smith (6)
Holmleigh Primary School, Hackney

Shark

It looks like scary, sharp, pointy teeth.
It sounds like a roar.
It feels like fluff.
It smells like a rock.
It looks like a shark.

Zion-Leigh Jonah Wallace (6)
Holmleigh Primary School, Hackney

Football

It looks like a pitch.
It sounds like people laughing.
It tastes like apples.
It smells like a fresh pitch.
It feels like a ball.

Raphael Opoku (6)
Holmleigh Primary School, Hackney

Lamborghini

It looks like a shark.
It sounds like a hawk.
It tastes like watermelon.
It smells like fresh flowers.
It feels like hard rock.

Ziyad Rawat (5)
Holmleigh Primary School, Hackney

Football

It looks like a ball in a hat
It sounds like rain
It tastes as good as pasta
It smells like an apple
It feels like a hard rock.

Haseeb Siddique (6)
Holmleigh Primary School, Hackney

Football

It looks like my friends are happy.
It sounds like a noisy football pitch.
It tastes like nothing.
It smells like a very good smell.

Essa Muruts (5)
Holmleigh Primary School, Hackney

Mountains

It looks like nature
It sounds like the wind
It tastes like hard rock
It smells like a nice breeze
It feels like soft snow.

Izan Fitzpatrick Salazar (5)
Holmleigh Primary School, Hackney

Ferrari

It looks like the sun
It sounds like *vroom!*
It tastes like water
It smells like an ice lolly
It feels warm.

Nathan Okulo Nugent (6)
Holmleigh Primary School, Hackney

My Mother

M y everything, without her I am nothing.
O nly you care for me whenever I am hurting
T he thought of you alone makes me happy.
H ere I am today, yesterday I was happy.
E mbracing me all the time, either night or day.
R aising me to be the best at it, come what may.

Michelle Oke (6)
Mayville Primary School, Leytonstone

Summer Animals And Flowers

Summer animals are so much fun
that sometimes you don't want to run.
There are bees that sometimes
hide in the trees
but others fly in the air
like they just don't care.
There are butterflies that fly high in the sky
that sometimes say goodbye.

Birds chirping and kids with
their ice lollies, slurping.
There are roses shining through
while daisies are too.
There are cows that say moo
and blossoms are blue.

It's a summer day, I hope the weather stays
and all the animals are having fun
now that summer has begun.

Carolina Valentina Pacheco Rich (7)
Mayville Primary School, Leytonstone

My Lovely Pets

My pets are lovely,
Sometimes they are really funny,
When I go on walks with my dogs,
They often find unfamiliar things under logs.
Unfortunately, my snakes cannot go
Out of their habitat,
I can only take them in my hands.
My lovely pets.

Amelia Niemira (7)
Mayville Primary School, Leytonstone

Kitten Love

K ey to happiness
I rresistibly cute
T oo fast
T erribly cuddly
E ntertaining
N ine lives.

Yousuf Muhammad (7)
Mayville Primary School, Leytonstone

My Little Sunshine

I wake up in the morning,
Hearing her voice coming along!
It sounds to me like a bird's song.

I hug her and feel her smell
And I take for my day power!
Oh, her smell is like a spring flower!
Her arms are like blankets around my shoulder
And I forgot if outside is colder.

Her bright face is like the sun in the morning
And nothing is, for me, boring.
My little sister makes me feel fine!
She is in my life,
My little sunshine!

Kimperly Boulou (7)
Noel Park Primary School, Wood Green

My Mysterious Creatures!

Every morning at half-past six,
I hear squeaks,
Hear the thumping of their feet.
It's time for them to eat!

With stubby toes and a cute little nose,
With floppy ears which strike fear.
Who are these mysterious creatures
Who have such cute features?
Why, they are my guinea pigs of course!

But when they are fed, it is time for bed
When they are awake, they repeat,
Asking for another treat!

Emilia Kasiak (7)
Noel Park Primary School, Wood Green

Dino Patrol

D id you see a dinosaur before?
I n the air and on the floor.
N othing ever gets in their way,
O nce they start to play.

P atrolling all day long,
A s they sing a song.
T ime passes by,
R unning to the sky.
O nly finding the way,
L earning every day.

Larisa Diana Dorcu (6)
Noel Park Primary School, Wood Green

Starlight

S taring at the midnight sky
T aking a look at the full moon bright
A s the wind gently passes by
R aising your hand to make a shadow against the light
L ooking at the stars
I t is very far
G alaxies you can see
H igh in the sky
T hey are very bright.

Jennica Sustines (7)
Noel Park Primary School, Wood Green

About Unicorns

U nder the rainbow, unicorns are flying.
N ice wings they have.
I f you see them, tell me.
C elebrate this day.
O n the other side of the world, there is Unicorn Land.
R eady to party in the clouds.
N ow they are looking at you from the sky.

Elisaveta Ilieva (7)
Noel Park Primary School, Wood Green

The Stars In The Sky

As stars shine in the sky,
There is a twinkle in your eye.
They guide your way every day
In the hard times.

As the time passes by, you will need a friend.
So they will guide and be your friend,
Every time you look in the bright sky!
The stars are your friends.

Liliana Ryzner (7)
Noel Park Primary School, Wood Green

White Dragons

D iabolical dragons stomping through the city,
R oaring loudly as they breathe fire!
A ngry feelings as they fly,
G igantic wings flapping into the sky.
O range scales on their body.
N aming every egg that hatches

Alex Harding (6)
Noel Park Primary School, Wood Green

Summer Is The Winner

Summer is hot,
And not cold,
You have food that is yummy,
So there is food in your tummy,
There are tasty dinners,
So summer is a winner!

Imani Ahmed (6)
Noel Park Primary School, Wood Green

Dippy The Diplodocus

D ippy is as huge as a blue whale with a brain as big as a fist.
I n herds it moves as slow as a slug across the land.
P lodding on its tree-trunk legs.
L ong, whip-like tail that swings at the speed of light.
O ther dinosaurs hear the noisy measuring tape snap!
D ippy's on the hunt for juicy leaves and he is always hungry.
O ver and over, the stones in his tummy grind up the leaves.
C hisel-like teeth to help him eat yummy leaves.
U nbelievably long neck that can reach tall trees.
S uper-sized sauropod, that's my favourite dinosaur.

Michele Zeolla (6)
Our Lady Of Lourdes Catholic Primary School, Finchley

Hungry Plant

I am not an animal.
I am a plant.
I like juicy flies.
I like to hunt.
Come, come to my green cup!
My slimy trap.
Where is my fly?
What am I?

Answer: A Venus flytrap.

Adela Mladenova (6)
Our Lady Of Lourdes Catholic Primary School, Finchley

Kitt And Me

At night, I can hear her purr
And I feel her soft golden fur

If my dream will allow
I might hear her meow

I stroke her gently, kiss her paws
She gives me cuddles, taps my nose

In the day when I'm at school
She'll chase a ball of wool

She'll pretend that it's a mouse
And chase it all over my house

I can't wait to come home and sit
And eat a KitKat with my cat Kitt

But she prefers milk and fish
And I say it's delish!

I love my cat.

Liana Dzadonova-Soskova (6)
Our Lady Of Lourdes Catholic Primary School, Finchley

The Cute, Snuggly Animals

Puppies are snuggly and cuddly,
They are fun to play with,
They are fuzzy, fluffy
And they are super duper cute!

Next up is a kitten,
They're playful to play with,
They're so snuggly and cute,
You can give them a small ping pong ball.

Next, we have a guinea pig,
Guinea pigs are so cute and a little bit fast,
They like to eat crunchy, orange carrots,
Yummy for a guinea pig,
They are super duper cute,
They are really fluffy and fussy.

The last animal is a unicorn,
Unicorns are a powerful magical animal,

Their mane is rainbow and super bright,
Same thing with their tail,
Their skin is white,
Fluffy, fuzzy skin,
They have ways to fly just like an alien,
But even better,
And that is the cute, snuggly poem,
And I loved it!

Houh Keskinbicak (7)
Randal Cremer Primary School, Hackney

A Dragon Poem

My dragon has veins on his wings like a zombie's brain.
It has sharp teeth like a ferocious buffalo.
It has sharp horns like a shark's tooth.
It has sharp claws like a dangerous dinosaur tooth.
The fire is like a building burning to ashes.
The eyes are like dots of fire.
The teeth are like very sharp knives.
The scales are like diamonds.

Finlay Dudek-Mahon (6)
Randal Cremer Primary School, Hackney

A Dragon Poem

My dragon is as strong as an ox
It has a spiky tail like thorns
Its marshmallows and rainbows
Are exquisite
It can shoot sweets out of its mouth
It can do kung fu
It's the king of all dragons
It can jump very high
It has ice
It can fly
It has foes
It has a jetpack!

Mani George Lister (6)
Randal Cremer Primary School, Hackney

A Dragon Poem

My dragon has wings
Which can make you shocked.
His face can make you get terrified.
His eyes look ferocious, like a ball
Who is ready to spear someone.
He has a moist body like a snake.
His fire bursts like water.

Kayden Tayvon Davis (6)
Randal Cremer Primary School, Hackney

A Dragon

My dragon is not fighting.
My dragon is strong.
My dragon is best.
My dragon likes meat.
My dragon never has showers.
My dragon has sharp teeth.
My dragon is light.

Yusuf Ahmed
Randal Cremer Primary School, Hackney

My Dragon

My dragon has four legs.
It can swim like a dog.
It has fire resistance.
It can fly.
It can run fast like a cheetah.
It's like it's walking.

Harry Paul Johns (5)
Randal Cremer Primary School, Hackney

My Dragon

My dragon has a tail that flicks from side to side like a crocodile's.
It has wing-like feathers five metres long.
Its eyes are as yellow as a crocodile's.

Mustafa Mohamed (6)
Randal Cremer Primary School, Hackney

My Dragon

My dragon has sharp teeth like a shark.
It has big fire when it's flying.
It has red eyes like it's evil.
It has claws like a crocodile.

Rafael Silva Amorim (6)
Randal Cremer Primary School, Hackney

What Am I?

I am as white as snow.
People use wood to make me.
I can be any colour.
People write on me.
I am used for loads of stuff.
What am I?

Olusegun Isaiah Olaifa (7)
Randal Cremer Primary School, Hackney

A Dragon

My dragon has wings like a zombie
It has sharp claws like a tiger
It has a sharp horn like an angry buffalo
It has a nose like a tiger.

Mariyah Rahman (6)
Randal Cremer Primary School, Hackney

Sunflower

Sunflowers smell like sweets.
Sunflowers look yellow and brown.
Sunflowers sound peaceful.
Sunflowers feel soft and smooth.

Khalid Ainab (6)
Seven Sisters Primary School, Tottenham

Carnations

Carnations smell like perfume.
Carnations look like butter.
Carnations sound unique.
Carnations feel like cotton candy.

Kerenza-Gabbie Alexiah Guei Nguiladjoe (6)
Seven Sisters Primary School, Tottenham

Carnations

Carnations smell like buttercream.
Carnations look colourful.
Carnations sound peaceful.
Carnations feel soft.

Ayaan Abdul (6)
Seven Sisters Primary School, Tottenham

Carnations

Carnations smell like perfume.
Carnations look frilly.
Carnations sound quiet.
Carnations feel silky.

Elalavin Toraman (6)
Seven Sisters Primary School, Tottenham

My Sunflower

My sunflower smells sweet.
My sunflower is calm.
My sunflower is soft.
My sunflower is lovely.

Emma Emmanuel (6)
Seven Sisters Primary School, Tottenham

Animal Poem

I am ferocious like a lion
And my colour is black and orange.
I am stripy as a buzzy bee and I have a tail.
I am as scary as a lion.
I am a carnivore.
I live in Africa.
I have sharp teeth and four legs.
What am I?

Answer: I am a tiger.

Miguel Dalfior-Milanese (6)
St Joseph's RC Primary School, Willesden

Animals

Vicious vulture
Flapping his wings.
Grumpy giraffes
Locating as they sing.
Shelley Shark
Swimming in the ocean.
Frightened fish
Out of the commotion.
Terrifying triceratops
Chasing his dinner.
Tired tiger
Sleeping and getting thinner.

Elijah Monu (5)
St Joseph's RC Primary School, Willesden

Animal Poem

It is white as snow and it is fluffy.
My animal eats carrots.
Moreover, it likes to hop all around.
Also, its tail looks like a bush.
It's so cute and it's quite small
And it has blue eyes.
What is it?

Answer: A bunny rabbit.

Leandra Aragao (6)
St Joseph's RC Primary School, Willesden

Animals

Lazy lions
Sleeping on the ground
Scary snakes
Slithering around
Munching monkeys
Laughing at the bear
Selfish skunks
They don't like to share
Colourful chameleon
Climbing up a tree
Pleasant pandas
As peaceful as the sea.

Joseph O'Connor-Macklen (6)
St Joseph's RC Primary School, Willesden

Animals

Feathery flamingo
Balancing on one leg
Mischievous monkey
Stole my friend's peg
Violent vulture
Eating the dead
Terrifying tiger
Sleeping on his bed
Slithering snake
As scary as a bat
Cute cats
Wearing silly hats.

Lexi Carrido (5)
St Joseph's RC Primary School, Willesden

Animals

Peaceful pandas
Munching their bamboo
Terrible tigers
Putting on their shoes
Courageous cats
Climbing up a tree
Malicious monkeys
Laughing at me
Excellent elephant
Punching his knee
Sleepy snakes
Swimming in the sea.

Adam Stachowicz (6)
St Joseph's RC Primary School, Willesden

Animals

Terrible tiger
Burning bright
Big brown bear
Eating honey in the night
Enormous elephant
Spraying water everywhere
Lazy lion
They don't play fair
Colourful chameleon
Climbing up a tree
Peaceful panda
Being free.

Mila Ndidi Aurora Johnson (6)
St Joseph's RC Primary School, Willesden

Animals

Excellent elephant
Stomping on the ground
Mischievous monkey
Making a loud sound
Lucky lion
Making loud roars
Big brown bear
Sleeping as he snores
Scaly snake
Slithering for one mile
Wet whale
Having a cheeky smile.

Cristian Alcantara (6)
St Joseph's RC Primary School, Willesden

Animals

Vicious vulture
Flapping his wings
Peaceful panda
Munching on a string
Grippy lizard
Changing its colour
Careful crocodiles
Munching on each other
Troubled tigers
Messing around
Racing rhinos
Sleeping on the ground.

Yafet Michael (6)
St Joseph's RC Primary School, Willesden

Animals

Fluffy flamingos,
Flying around.
Lazy lions,
Lying on the ground.
Crunching crocodiles,
Live in the sea.
Pleasant pandas,
Nibbling on a pea.
Hungry hippos,
Like to eat meat.
Kind kangaroos
On the Australian street.

Zenaye Richards (6)
St Joseph's RC Primary School, Willesden

Animals

Vicious vulture
Flapping his wings
Busy birds
Flying as they sing
Lucky lion
Wiggling his tail
Generous giraffe
His spots are very pale
Munching monkeys
Swinging on the rope
Peaceful pandas
Falling down a slope.

Kojo Agbugba (6)
St Joseph's RC Primary School, Willesden

Animals

Jiggling jellyfish
Swimming as it stings
Terrible tigers
Roar and spring
Lucky lions
Asleep on the ground
Black bats
Wandering all around
Big bad bears
Looking for food
Cheeky cheetahs
In their big bad moods.

Angel Mabag (6)
St Joseph's RC Primary School, Willesden

Animals

Peaceful panda
Eating bamboo
Zigzagged zebras
Galloping in the zoo
Jiggling jellyfish
Swimming in the sea
Buzzing bees
Chasing after me
Troubled tiger
Pouncing on its paws
Lucky lions
With big sharp claws.

Diane Omas (6)
St Joseph's RC Primary School, Willesden

Animals

Lazy lions
Hunting while they crawl
Gentle giraffes
Do have jaws
Terrifying tigers
Sleeping on the ground
Cheeky cheetahs
Sly as they run around
Silly snakes
Circling on rocks
Busy bears
Snoring on blocks.

Zackary Resurreccion Geluz Silva (6)
St Joseph's RC Primary School, Willesden

Animals

Stinky skunk
Chasing around
Cheeky cheetah
Scratching the ground
Lucky lion
With pointy, sharp claws
Terrible tigers
With big, brown paws
Pleasant pandas
Munching on bamboo
Baby bears
Washing with shampoo.

Nicole Ferreira (6)
St Joseph's RC Primary School, Willesden

Animals

Lazy leopard
Chasing after me
Peaceful panda
Munching on a pea
Sleepy snake
Sleeping on the ground
Terrible tiger
Sprinting all around
Washing whale
Swimming in the sea
Lazy lion
Staring at a bee.

Remy Kyerematen (6)
St Joseph's RC Primary School, Willesden

Animals

Lazy lion
Running around
Terrible tigers
Lying on the ground
Malicious monkey
Swinging on a tree
Cheeky chameleon
Chomping on a pea
Baby bear
Playing with food
Peaceful pandas
Not in a good mood.

Zuzanna Baran (6)
St Joseph's RC Primary School, Willesden

Animals

Gentle giraffe
Tall as a tree
Peaceful panda
Munching on a pea
Lazy lion
Swinging his tail
Sneaky snake
Shining its scales
Troubled tiger
With sharp claws
Shocking shark
Vicious teeth and jaws.

Sara Bereket (6)
St Joseph's RC Primary School, Willesden

An Animal Poem

It has a white tummy and black paws.
It has cute ears and cute paws.
It swings like a monkey on a tree.
It is as soft as a teddy.
It eats bamboo and it lives in a forest.
What is it?

Answer: A panda.

Molly Noonan-Conneely (6)
St Joseph's RC Primary School, Willesden

What Am I?

I am tiny as a little baby
I have sharp teeth like a knife
I live in a happy house like people
I eat carrots as crunchy as celery sticks
I can hop as high as a fence.
What am I?

Answer: A rabbit.

Jean Alexander Calva Angeles (6)
St Joseph's RC Primary School, Willesden

What Am I?

I eat crunchy bones like a cookie
I squeak like a mouse when I'm scared
I live in a happy house like people
I am white and black like a zebra
I am sweet and cute.
What am I?

Answer: A puppy.

Sarah Lukowska (6)
St Joseph's RC Primary School, Willesden

Animal Poem

I have yellow and brown spots.
I have a lots of spots like a leopard.
I am as tall as a tree.
I eat green grass and it is fresh.
I live in the big zoo.
What am I?

Answer: I am a giraffe.

Liliana Czapska (6)
St Joseph's RC Primary School, Willesden

What Am I?

I live with people like kids
I eat meat like lollipops
I scratch when dogs are next to me
I am not as small as a mouse
I am very fluffy like a pretty puppy.
What am I?

Answer: A kitten.

Chanelle Cadigal Bernardo (6)
St Joseph's RC Primary School, Willesden

Animal Poem

I am a clever carnivore.
I eat small animals for food.
I am as terrifying as a tiger.
I am orange like a ferocious fire.
I run like a cat in the wild.
What am I?

Answer: I am a fox.

Tristan Mingo Corpuz (6)
St Joseph's RC Primary School, Willesden

What Am I?

I live in the jungle like a terrible tiger
I eat meat as yummy as a lollipop
I am not as small as a mouse
I have sharp, terrible teeth like a knife.
What am I?

Answer: I am a lion.

Bethany Elfy (6)
St Joseph's RC Primary School, Willesden

The Parrot

Squawking loudly in the sky,
Squawking very high.
Colourful feathers,
As bright as a rainbow.

Squawking and talking,
A very yellow beak.
Colourful feathers,
Flapping in the air.

Taira Miankanina (6)
St Joseph's RC Primary School, Willesden

Riddle Poem

I am ferocious like a grizzly bear
My colours are black and orange
I roar like a lion
I like meat because I am a carnivore
I live in the jungle.
What am I?

Answer: A tiger.

Julio Peixoto Jr (6)
St Joseph's RC Primary School, Willesden

What Am I?

I live by the lake like a swan
I am pink like candyfloss
I have skinny legs
Like a scary, scary skeleton
I have small wings like a bluebird.
What am I?

Answer: A flamingo.

Bezawit-Elen Berhane (6)
St Joseph's RC Primary School, Willesden

The Elephant

Stomping his feet loudly,
Stomping very hard.
Big trunk swinging sideways,
Swinging side to side.
As big as a tower?
As heavy as a school.
Elephant is stomping,
Stomping very hard.

Roxy Ayisi (5)
St Joseph's RC Primary School, Willesden

What Am I?

I live in a house as tall as a tree
I eat fresh food and milk like a baby
I like to play with a bouncy ball like a boy
I am as fluffy as a pillow.
What am I?

Answer: A kitten.

Althea Megan Matysik (5)
St Joseph's RC Primary School, Willesden

The Hamster

Spinning in my wheel,
Spinning all around.
As fast as a cheetah,
Spinning all around.

The hamster has fur,
The hamster is soft.
The hamster is cute,
The hamster in a wheel.

Lily-Sue O'Dea Nolan (6)
St Joseph's RC Primary School, Willesden

What Am I?

I have bushy hair like an afro.
I have furry skin like a cat.
I have a long tail like Rapunzel's hair.
I live in the jungle as green as Shrek.
What am I?

Answer: A lion.

Chloe Pereira de Jesus (6)
St Joseph's RC Primary School, Willesden

The Puppy

Playing with my stick
The stick goes very far.
Running to catch my stick
It is very fun.

Barking loudly
Barking as I run.
The stick goes very far
Playing with my stick.

Marcel Oliwkiewicz (6)
St Joseph's RC Primary School, Willesden

Animal Poem

I live in a hive.
I like honey like Winnie the Pooh.
I fly like a beautiful busy butterfly.
I am yellow and black.
I hurt you when I sting.
What am I?

Answer: A bee.

Mia-Rose Berry (5)
St Joseph's RC Primary School, Willesden

Animal Poem

I am as scary as a bear.
I live in the jungle.
Sometimes my roar is as loud as a car horn.
My face is full of fur.
I have a long tail.
What am I?

Answer: I am a lion.

Ionna Braganca (6)
St Joseph's RC Primary School, Willesden

The Horse

Galloping very fast,
Galloping in the race.
Galloping on the grass,
Galloping quickly.

Galloping forward,
Galloping to the end.
Galloping very fast,
Galloping quickly.

Anaise Toyin Amiyah Allen (6)
St Joseph's RC Primary School, Willesden

What Am I?

I have a tiny tail like a small dot.
I live in a happy cage like a jail.
I eat crunchy carrots like a rabbit.
I'm as quiet as a mouse.
What am I?

Answer: A hamster.

Oliwer Kwasniak (6)
St Joseph's RC Primary School, Willesden

The Dragon

Breathing hot fire,
As hot as the sun.
Great flames of fire,
Coming from his mouth.

Sharp spikes on his head,
Sharp as nails.
His teeth are sharp,
Sharp as a pencil.

Thiery Daisy (6)
St Joseph's RC Primary School, Willesden

A Dolphin

Jumping up and down,
Splashing in the sea.
Smooth as silk,
It moves in the air.

Jumping up and down,
Twirling in the air.
Flipping up and down,
Swirling in the air.

Bleu-Taneil Henry-Skye (6)
St Joseph's RC Primary School, Willesden

The Cat

Whiskers are very long,
A long, stripy tail.
Drinking lots of milk,
Big brown eyes.

Purring very loudly,
Looking all around.
Playing with the ball,
In the garden.

Amelia-Mae Norwood (6)
St Joseph's RC Primary School, Willesden

What Am I?

I eat nectar like sweet honey
I have blue eyes like water
I have wonderful wings like a rainbow
I have cute colours like glitter.
What am I?

Answer: A butterfly.

Renee Labiran (6)
St Joseph's RC Primary School, Willesden

What Am I?

I climb trees like a monkey
I live in a big house with people
I have small claws like commas
I eat milky milk like a little baby.
What am I?

Answer: A kitten.

Isabella Lynn-Lee-Henningham (6)
St Joseph's RC Primary School, Willesden

What Am I?

I live in a jungle as green as grass
I eat twigs as crunchy as a carrot
I am quiet like a mouse
I am white and black like a zebra.
What am I?

Answer: A panda.

Amelia Grace Myers (6)
St Joseph's RC Primary School, Willesden

Animal Poem

I am as small as a slimy slug.
I am a light green reptile.
I look like a little crocodile.
I have a tail as long as a tall tree.
What am I?

Answer: A lizard.

Maxymilian Olczyk-Pinto (6)
St Joseph's RC Primary School, Willesden

What Am I?

I eat meat like a lazy lion
I live in the jungle like a zebra
I have paws like a terrifying tiger
I can laugh like a crazy clown
What am I?

Answer: A hyena.

Antoni Sagalski (6)
St Joseph's RC Primary School, Willesden

The Panther

Prowling in the dark,
Prowling all around,
A big black cat,
As black as night.

Prowling in the jungle,
Prowling all around,
A big black cat,
Sharp claws.

Da'Shaun Brown (5)
St Joseph's RC Primary School, Willesden

The Kitten

A small ball of fur,
A small little head.
Small furry paws,
Long whiskers.

Chasing the mice,
All around the room.
Purring loudly,
Very happy kitten.

Urte Raubaite (5)
St Joseph's RC Primary School, Willesden

The Spider

Eight long legs,
All moving quickly,
Spinning a web,
Very quickly.

The web is long,
The web is sticky,
The web is patterned,
The spider in the web.

Sergio Santos Filho (5)
St Joseph's RC Primary School, Willesden

The Shark

The shark is in the sea
Deep, deep down
The shark has sharp teeth.

The shark is in the sea
Looking for some food
The shark has fins
And swims very fast.

Marie Gilera (6)
St Joseph's RC Primary School, Willesden

The Peacock

Beautiful, colourful,
Open out wide,
Beautiful colours,
Like the rainbow,
The peacock stands tall,
The feathers are open,
Open and close,
Lots of colours.

Roukai Edwards (6)
St Joseph's RC Primary School, Willesden

Penguin Poem

I live in Antarctica.
I eat floppy fish.
I am a bird.
I like to swim.
I am black and white like a zebra.
What am I?

Answer: I am a penguin.

Karina Firlej (6)
St Joseph's RC Primary School, Willesden

The Zebra

The zebra is stripy,
Black and white.
The zebra eats leaves
From the jungle.

The zebra has a long tail
And big eyes.
The zebra walks in the jungle.

Janiah Hall (5)
St Joseph's RC Primary School, Willesden

Tiger

My tiger has long stripes, long as the pipes in my class.
His teeth are sharp like my pencil.
His ears point up when he is hungry.
Be careful - he can eat you!

James Koroma (6)
St Joseph's RC Primary School, Willesden

The Cheetah

Spotty all over
The cheetah is fast
He has a long tail
With sharp claws

In the jungle
The cheetah moves fast
He is everywhere.

Colm O'Brien (6)
St Joseph's RC Primary School, Willesden

Jesus

J erusalem, that is the town where I grew up
E aster, that was the day of my resurrection
S ins are washed away by my blood
U nderstand you are loved by me
S o whoever believes in me will have eternal life.

Daniel Lahuk (7)
St Jude & St Paul's CE Primary School, London

What Am I?

I eat fish.
I dive at 300mph.
I have sharp eyes.
The first letter of my name is 'P'.
What am I?

Answer: I'm a peregrine falcon.

Teniola Aluko (7)
St Jude & St Paul's CE Primary School, London

Playing In The Park

I like to swing, I like to hide.
I like to run, I like to slide.
I like to spin, I like to win.
I like to play on a sunny day.

Kaylie Evans (7)
St Jude & St Paul's CE Primary School, London

Mystery Poem

I am nice
I like to play
I love parks
I love balls
I love to bark
I love to wag my tail and
I love to pant when I'm hot.
What am I?

Answer: A dog, that's what!

Tina David (7)
St Mary's CE Primary School, Stoke Newington

Colours All Around Us

I am the colour of the fire engines
And hearts,
Also strawberries and apples,
What am I?

Answer: Red.

I am the colour of the sun,
Buttercups and lemons.
What am I?

Answer: Yellow.

I am mixed with red and yellow,
Also a fruit, lava and sunset.
What am I?

Answer: Orange.

Tomisin Okotore (10)
The Holmewood School, Barnet

A Mouse And A Flea

There was a mouse in the house
Who loved cheese and hated peas

But the fleas took the keys
So he couldn't go out in the breeze

One day, the mouse pleased the fleas
Who gave him the keys

So he went out to have some fun
In the big bright sun!

Raafay Yusuf (7)
Upton Meadows Primary School, Upton

Nature

F lower
L ovely
O live
W onderful
E xciting
R eading
S eeds.

Nehal Ba Omar (7)
Upton Meadows Primary School, Upton

Pets

P laying with them is fun
E very day, they are cute
T hat's always true
S ee for yourself and get one!

Megan Wilson (6)
Vita Et Pax School, Southgate

Crocodile

C rocodiles creep down the river
R oaming to find their prey
O n their way for a morning swim
C olossal teeth snapping its prey
O bviously, they always swim
D ancing elegantly on the waterhole
I n the water, they eat all day long
L ong tails for defending from predators
E very day, they eat and swim like a hungry shark.

Kiaan Mukherjee (6)
Wimbledon Common Preparatory School, Wimbledon

Cheetah Wins

C unning speed, a cheetah has every time
H e zooms here and there, hunting animals
E ating animals with deep blood
E ach day, biting, scrapping animals and winning
T eeth sharp
A nd legs ready to run, can you
H ear his powerful crunch?

Atharva Sharma (6)
Wimbledon Common Preparatory School, Wimbledon

Zebra

Z igzagging across the savannah
E very zebra is black and white
B eautiful, long stripes
R unning around the African plains
A lert to being hunted by lions.

Isaiah van der Meer (7)
Wimbledon Common Preparatory School, Wimbledon

Zebra

Z ipping through the deserted desert
E ndangered species
B ig, muffled animal
R aging hot fur
A t night, zebras sleep in their comfy beds.

Kevin Ruo (7)
Wimbledon Common Preparatory School, Wimbledon

Young Writers Information

We hope you have enjoyed reading this book – and that you will continue to in the coming years.

If you're a young writer who enjoys reading and creative writing, or the parent of an enthusiastic poet or story writer, do visit our website **www.youngwriters.co.uk**. Here you will find free competitions, workshops and games, as well as recommended reads, a poetry glossary and our blog.

If you would like to order further copies of this book, or any of our other titles, then please give us a call or visit **www.youngwriters.co.uk**.

Young Writers
Remus House
Coltsfoot Drive
Peterborough
PE2 9BF
(01733) 890066
info@youngwriters.co.uk

@YoungWritersUK @YoungWritersCW